Leading Lady

MOTHER TERESA

By: Jill Wheeler

Published by Abdo & Daughters, 6535 Cecilia Circle, Edina, Minnesota 55439.

Library bound edition distributed by Rockbottom Books, Pentagon Tower, P.O. Box 36036, Minneapolis, Minnesota 55435.

Printed in the United States.

Cover Photo: Archive Photos
Inside Photos: Bettman Newsphoto 4, 10, 15, 23, 28 & 31
                 Archive Photos 19 & 26

Edited by Rosemary Wallner

LIBRARY OF CONGRESS CATALOGING-IN-PUBLICATION DATA

Wheeler, Jill C., 1964-
    Mother Teresa / written by Jill C. Wheeler.
        p. cm. — (Leading Ladies)
    Summary: A brief biography of the nun who has heightened the consciousness of the world to helping the poor.
    ISBN 1-56239-119-4
    1. Teresa, Mother, 1910- -- Juvenile literature. 2. Missionaries of Charity -- Biography -- Juvenile literature. 3. Nuns -- India-Calcutta -- Biography -- Juvenile literature 4. Calcutta (India) -- Biography -- Juvenile literature. [1. Teresa, Mother, 1910- . 2. Nuns.] I. Title. II. Series.
BX4406.5Z8W54 1992   271'.97--dc20   92-16675
                                              [B]

International Standard Book Number:	Library of Congress Catalog Card Number:
1-56239-119-4	92-16675

TABLE OF CONTENTS

Mother Teresa attending the Right to Life convention in Washington D.C.

MOTHER TO THE WORLD

On a cold day in December 1979, a tiny woman stepped off a plane in Oslo, Norway. Despite the cold, she was wearing only a short jacket, sandals and a thin white sari with blue trim. A sari is the clothing worn by the women of India. A cross was pinned at her left shoulder.

A parade greeted the woman as she passed through the streets of Oslo. People waved and shouted her name, but she remained quiet. Later, she mounted a platform to receive the world's most famous award. At only five feet in height, she could barely see over the podium. The broad smile on her tanned and wrinkled face radiated warmth throughout the room.

The award was the Nobel Peace Prize. It is given each year to a person who people believe has done much to advance the cause of peace. Most people who receive the award are active in politics.

This time, however, was an exception. The woman was Mother Teresa, founder of the Missionaries of Charity. She had traveled thousands of miles from her home in India, to be recognized for her work in helping feed and care for poor people. The members of the Nobel committee gave her the award because they knew people sometimes go to war because they are hungry. Even so, Mother Teresa said she did not think she deserved the award.

"Personally, I am unworthy," she said. "I accept in the name of the poor, because I believe that by giving me the prize they have recognized the presence of the poor in the world." After she had made her remarks, she received a prize of $190,000. She quietly told the crowd that she would use the money to help the poor.

A VILLAGE IN MACEDONIA

Mother Teresa was born Agnes Gonxha (Gohn-ja) Bojaxhiu (Boy-ya-jee-oo) on August 27, 1910, in the village of Skopje (Sko-pee-ay) in Macedonia.

Macedonia is now called Yugoslavia. The new baby had an older sister Age and brother Lazar to welcome her.

Agnes's father was a contractor named Nikola. He was active in politics. He often met with other men to talk about making their country better. Nikola loved his family, and their home often echoed with laughter.

Agnes's mother was named Drana. She was a very religious woman and she passed that trait on to her children. She enjoyed staying home with them and teaching them to love one another. Once, she even took a sick woman into the family's home and nursed her there because the woman had no one to help her.

Everything changed one night when Agnes was ten years old. Her father had returned from a political meeting. Suddenly, he crumpled to the ground. The family rushed him to a hospital, but he died there in surgery. The family always wondered if someone had poisoned Nikola because of his political beliefs.

At first, Drana didn't know what to do. How could the family get enough money to live now that her husband was gone? But Drana was very strong and determined. She started an embroidery business to make money. She also made sure the children continued their schooling and attended church regularly.

Agnes loved to go to church. She found it comforting to celebrate Mass every morning. She also sang in the church choir, and played the accordion and the mandolin. In the afternoons, she and her family would return to church for several hours. In the evening at home, they would pray once more with their rosaries.

Young Agnes also loved to hear stories of missionaries in far-away lands. She was especially interested in how church people were helping the poor in India. By the time she was fifteen, Agnes was thinking about becoming a nun so she could help the poor people of India, too.

TO IRELAND!

By the time Agnes finished high school, she had decided it was time to leave to become a missionary nun. Her decision surprised her brother. He asked how someone as fun-loving as her would want to be a nun. "How could you, a girl like you, become a nun?" he wrote to her. She wrote back, "You think you are so important, as an official serving the king. Well, I am an official too, serving the King of the whole world. Which one of us is right?"

Agnes never doubted her decision to become a nun. She said it was because God had called her. Many years later she would say, "I've never doubted even for a second that I've done the right thing; it was the will of God. It was His choice."

Agnes wanted to become a member of the order known as the Sisters of Loreto. The Sisters of Loreto had been missionaries in India for more than one hundred years.

Mother Teresa (left) and members of her order kneel in prayer.

Yet to become a Loreto sister, Agnes knew she would have to leave her home and family forever. She wrote to the Sisters at their convent in Ireland and asked if she could join them. They said she could.

Shortly after she turned eighteen, Agnes boarded a train for France and left her family. She would never see her mother or sister again. In France, she took a ship to the British Isles and then another train to the Rathfarnham Abbey near Dublin, Ireland. She stayed in the Abbey for six weeks learning about the Sisters of Loreto. She was called a postulant, meaning "one who knocks on the door". One of her first tasks at the Abbey was to learn English.

Soon Agnes took another ship to Darjeeling, India. In this beautiful city at the foot of the Himalayas Mountains, she became a novice. That means "a new Sister". Now she began to study the Bible more and prepare to do God's work. She learned the languages native Indians speak. She taught local children when she was not studying.

Nearly three years went by. The time had come for Agnes to take her first vows toward becoming a nun. She participated in a ceremony where she vowed to live a simple life, love God with all her heart and obey God and her superiors. She also chose a new name to signify her new life. She chose the name Teresa, after another tiny nun who had died long ago. That Teresa had been called the "little flower of Jesus. " Like Agnes, she too believed she could serve God through even the smallest tasks.

TEACHING AT ST. MARY'S

Sister Teresa was ready to leave for her true mission. At last she was going to Calcutta, the city she had dreamed of for so many years. However, instead of helping the poor, her superiors told her she must teach at St. Mary's High School.

St. Mary's was located in the middle of the Moti Jheel (Mo-tee Jeel) slum. Inside its walls were beautiful gardens and quiet.

Outside, there was the terrible smell of the slums and the noise of thousands of people. After teaching history and geography during the day, Sister Teresa would go to her room in the nearby convent and stare out the window at the slums below.

She saw hundreds of homeless people, many naked, starving and covered with oozing sores. People slept in the streets under cardboard boxes or gasoline cans. The air was filled with the stench of sewage, the smoke from hundreds of cooking fires and the cries of hungry children. Many of the homeless people were dying, yet sometimes no one even noticed when they died.

Sister Teresa wanted to help the people she saw, but her superiors did not like it when the nuns left the convent. It wasn't safe for women to wander in the slums alone, they said. Besides, they added, the Sisters took care of some widows and orphans inside St. Mary's walls.

Sister Teresa taught at St. Mary's for nearly 20 years. During that time, she took her final vows to become a true Sister of Loreto. She even became the principal of St. Mary's. She enjoyed teaching and was popular with her students. Yet she felt something was missing. On a September day in 1946, she discovered what that was.

HEARING GOD'S CALL

Every year, each Sister of Loreto took a retreat to spend time alone praying and meditating. When Sister Teresa's turn came, she took the night train to Darjeeling. As the train clacked through the night, her mind whirled about what she could do to help the poor people she saw from her window each day. Suddenly she knew. She must give up the Loreto order and go into the streets to help the poorest of the poor.

Later she said she felt her decision was an order from God. "The message was quite clear," she said. "I was to leave the convent and help the poor while living among them," she said. She realized it would be difficult.

Nuns were not allowed to live outside the convent. She would have to get permission from the Pope himself.

Pope Pius XII (Pacelli), 1938-1958.

As soon as she returned to Calcutta, Sister Teresa
went to the Archbishop of Calcutta. She told him what
God had ordered her to do. She wanted the Archbishop to ask the Pope if she could leave the convent.
The Archbishop did not agree to her request right
away. He said he needed to make sure that was what
God wanted for Sister Teresa. He also said he wor-
ried about her safety.

It took two years for Sister Teresa to convince the
Archbishop that her plan to live and work among the
poor was right. Finally, the Archbishop took her plea
to the Pope. In 1948, the Pope gave Sister Teresa
permission to live outside the convent.

Even with the Pope's permission, Sister Teresa said
the decision was difficult. "Leaving Loreto was for me
the greatest sacrifice, the most difficult thing I have
ever done," she said. "It was a lot more difficult than
leaving my family and country to become a nun.
Loreto was everything to me."

Immediately, Sister Teresa went to Patna, India, to get medical training from the American Medical Missionaries. She knew she would need this training to help the slum dwellers of Calcutta. She also exchanged her nun's robe and head covering, called a habit, for a white sari with blue trim. Sister Teresa wanted to look like the people she helped. She vowed to beg for her food like the poor and eat only rice and salt like they ate. But the missionaries at Patna told her she must eat well enough to keep up her strength to do God's work.

When she returned to Calcutta, she went out into the slums alone. She was a thirty-eight-year-old woman with less than a dollar in her pocket and no place to live. All she had was the faith that God would provide everything she needed. Soon, a priest friend found a man who offered Mother Teresa a room in his house to live for free. Her mission had begun.

HELPING ONE PERSON
AT A TIME

Sister Teresa knew she could not help everyone in the slum. She decided instead to help those closest to her. Since she had been a teacher, she began with the children. She found a patch of open ground and began drawing letters of the alphabet in the dirt with a stick. A group of children quickly gathered to watch. At first there were only a few children who wanted to learn. Then the group grew until she was teaching hundreds of children.

As Sister Teresa taught them, she also took care of them. She asked people to give her soap and then used it to wash the children. She told them how God loved them. The children grew to love Sister Teresa's warm hugs and ready smiles.

Some people began to take notice of Sister Teresa's work. People began giving gifts of food, medicine, supplies for her school and milk for the children to drink.

The only woman called a saint in her lifetime, Mother Teresa, is distributing the only Christmas present her years in Calcutta have taught her is worthwhile- a pound of rice and a blanket.

One night, Sister Teresa opened her door to find one of her former students from St. Mary's. The young woman asked if she could work with Sister Teresa.

Within two years, Sister Teresa had so much help the Pope told her she could start a new order of nuns. Sister Teresa called this new order the Missionaries of Charity. She became the leader, or Mother Superior. Her name became Mother Teresa.

Mother Teresa had strict rules for herself and the people who worked with her. They could own no more than three saris, a mattress to sleep on, a pair of sandals and a bucket for washing. "In order to understand and help those who have nothing, we must live like them," Mother Teresa said.

She also asked her Sisters to take a fourth vow in addition to the three standard vows. They must promise to serve only the poor and to receive no pay for what they did. "A Missionary of Charity must be a missionary of love," Mother Teresa told her followers.

"She must be full of love in her own soul and spread that same love to the souls of others."

Life as a Sister was hard. The nuns got up at 4:30 each morning, worshipped and then ate a meager breakfast. They worked in the streets all morning and then returned to the house they lived in for lunch. After lunch, there were more prayers, a short rest and then more work in the streets. Evenings, the nuns had some time for games and singing before evening prayers and finally, bedtime.

Mother Teresa believed her nuns should work hard and also have some fun. She often stayed up late, getting just a few hours of sleep a night. She felt there was so much to do she didn't have the time to rest.

Soon the house they had been living in was too small. With the help of a local priest and the Archbishop of Calcutta, the Missionaries of Charity were able to buy a larger house. The house, on Lower Circular Road, is still the headquarters for the Missionaries of Charity.

DIGNITY FOR THE DYING

In 1952, Mother Teresa began another project. It bothered her to see how poor people were treated when they died. Most died in the street because hospitals refused to care for poor people. Once, Mother Teresa found a dying woman in the street and brought her to a hospital. The hospital did not want to take her, but Mother Teresa refused to leave until the woman was given a bed so she could die comfortably.

Mother Teresa decided Calcutta needed a special place where poor people could die with dignity. She begged local authorities for a few rooms. The police told her she could have part of an old temple. After cleaning the filthy rooms in the temple, Mother Teresa and her helpers began bringing dying people there. She called her new mission Nirmal Hriday (Nir-mul Hree-day). In Indian, it means "the place of pure light."

Nirmal Hriday quickly became a bustling place. Some of the people who were brought there off the streets died, but others got well. All received kind and loving care.

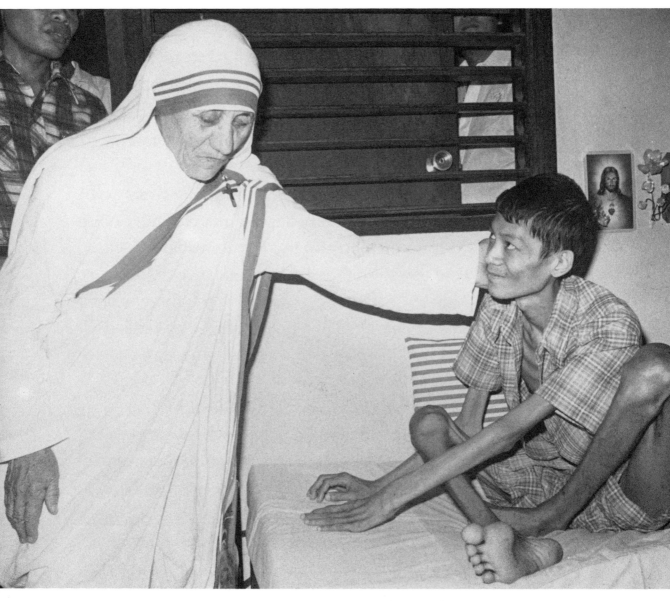

*Nobel Peace Prize winner Mother Teresa, comforts a polio victim
at a home for the destitude, in Manila.*

"We want to make them feel that they are wanted and loved, that they are somebody special," Mother Teresa said. Often the smell in the rooms was gagging, but Mother Teresa and her helpers did not appear to notice.

Some people were upset with what Mother Teresa was doing. She was Roman Catholic, but many of the people she helped were members of the Hindu religion. Some Hindus were afraid Mother Teresa was trying to get dying people to change their religion. They threw stones and shouted at her. Finally, a police officer was called in to get her and her Sisters out of the temple.

The officer was amazed when he saw what Mother Teresa was doing. He told the people who were complaining, "I promised I would get that woman out of here. And I shall. But first you must get your mothers and sisters to do the work these nuns are doing." Finally, the people learned the nuns had taken care of a dying Hindu priest no one else would help. After that, they did not complain anymore.

HELPING THE CHILDREN
AND THE OUTCASTS

Another problem that disturbed Mother Teresa was the many orphaned and dying children in the streets of Calcutta. Many parents would leave their babies on trash heaps to die because they could not afford to feed them. If the children survived, they ran wild in the streets and suffered from sickness and starvation. Mother Teresa wanted a place where all children would be welcome and cared for.

In 1953, Mother Teresa opened Shishu Bhavan (Shee-shu Bah-ven), a home for dying and abandoned children. Volunteers, policemen and social workers brought the children they found to the home. Some were babies who had been left outside to die. Others were older children covered with dirt, sores and lice. Many of the children were sick, crippled or retarded. Mother Teresa would turn no child away.

Mother Teresa, among the needy of Calcutta.

At Shishu Bhavan, Mother Teresa made sure all children knew they were loved. She nursed some back to health and eased the pain of those who were dying. Some went back to their families. Others were adopted. Still others lived in the home until they were old enough to marry and start their own families.

The Missionaries of Charity now were helping dying people and abandoned children. But for Mother Teresa, it was not enough. In 1957, she opened another special place to help people who suffered from leprosy. Leprosy is a feared disease in India that causes ugly sores. People who have it, called lepers, are outcasts. No one wants to be near them, so they spend their days begging in the streets.

Mother Teresa set up a special clinic for lepers and welcomed them with open arms. She helped them learn a trade to earn money. She provided them with medicine. Some were cured of the terrible disease. Over the years, the clinic and a leper village started by Mother Teresa have helped thousands of lepers and their families.

*"Saint of the Slums", Mother Teresa, Roman
Catholic nun, in Calcutta, India.*

A WORLD OF LOVE

Mother Teresa's work continued to grow. In 1963, a group of men called the Missionary Brothers of Charity were formed to help the women of the Missionaries of Charity. In 1965, the Missionaries of Charity received permission from the church to set up their first operation outside India. They opened a mission to help poor people in Venezuela.

Since then, the Missionaries of Charity have helped people in Australia, the Middle East, Europe and North America. They help by setting up clinics, schools, free food distribution centers and homes for sick and dying people. There are even Missionaries of Charity centers in some cities in the United States.

Mother Teresa makes a point of visiting all the places where her order has centers. She travels so much, the government of India gave her a pass to fly free on the country's airline. Everywhere she goes, she is welcomed with smiles and hugs. "People are not hungry just for bread," she says. "They are hungry for love."

GOD WILL PROVIDE

Mother Teresa's work is supported by donations from many people. She believes God will provide what she needs to carry out her work. When she needs something, she asks God to give it to her. Her prayers have been answered many times. Once she wanted to start a new children's home in an Indian town but she did not have enough money. Then she learned the government of the Philippines had given her an award. The award came with just the right amount of money she needed for her children's home.

Another time in London, Mother Teresa wanted to buy a house to start a mission. Her followers began collecting donations. By the time they were done, she had enough money to buy the house. Yet another time, the Pope visited her. Before leaving India, he gave her the car he had used while in the country. Mother Teresa raffled off the car and made enough money to build a leper village.

Mother Teresa's work has been recognized by many people over the years. She has received the highest honor presented by her adopted country of India. She also has been recognized by the Pope, the United States and Great Britain. She accepts all awards in the name of the poor. She gives the prize money to help feed the hungry, heal the sick, and spread love and understanding.

Pope John Paul II holds hands with Mother Teresa during his visit to Calcutta in 1986.

CARRYING OUT GOD'S WORK

Mother Teresa is more than eighty years old now, but she still works every day. In late 1991, she was hospitalized for pneumonia. The doctors said she needed to eat better food if she wanted to avoid getting sick again.

The Missionaries of Charity have come a long way since Sister Teresa first stepped out into the slums of Calcutta. Today, her order helps feed more than 7,000 people in Calcutta every day. There are more than 100 Missionaries of Charity centers in India alone. And white and blue saris can be seen helping the poor from England to Australia and the U.S. to South America.

Perhaps most importantly, Mother Teresa has shown that one person can make a difference.